The Big Book Of Jokes

Katherine Hennessy   Daniel Hennessy

Sameul Hennessy

The Hennessy Entertainment Company

The Big Book of Jokes / by Daniel Hennessy & Samuel Hennessy & Katherine Hennessy

ISBN 978-1-989621-14-1 (Print)

ISBN 978-1-989621-15-8 (E-book)

1. Wit and humor, Juvenile. 2. English wit and humor. I. Daniel Hennessy & Samuel Hennessy & Katherine Hennessy, authors.

The Hennessy Entertainment Company | HennessyEnt.com

To everyone who makes people smile.

1

Knock Knock Jokes

Knock, knock.

Who's there?

A little old lady.

A little old lady who?

Cool, I didn't know you could yodel.

Knock, knock.

Who's there?

Adore.

Adore who?

Adore is between you and me so please open up.

Knock, knock.

Who's there?

Boo.

Boo who?

Don't cry.

Knock, knock.

Who's there?

A pile up.

A pile up who?

Eww, that's just gross.

Knock, knock.

Who's there?

Cockle doodle.

Cockle doodle who?

Guess it's time to wake up.

Knock, knock.

Who's there?

Control Freak.

Contro—

Okay, now you say, "Control freak who?"

Knock, knock.

Who's there?

Interrupting zombie.

Inter—

BRAAAAAAINS.

Knock, knock.

Who's there?

Interrupting sloth.

Interrupting sloth who?

(Count to 5 silently, then): Sloooooooooth.

Knock, knock.

Who's there?

Cotton.

Cotton who?

Cotton the door, please open it and let me out.

Knock, knock.

Who's there?

Cows go.

Cows go who?

No, cows go moo.

Knock, knock.

Who's there?

Déjà.

Déjà who?

Knock, knock.

Knock, knock.

Who's there?

Dime.

Dime who?

Dime for another knock-knock joke.

Knock, knock.

Who's there?

Disguise.

Disguise who?

Disguise falling, disguise falling.

Knock, knock.

Who's there?

Dishes

Dishes who?

Dishes the police, open up!

Knock, knock.

Who's there?

Dismay.

Dismay who?

Dismay seem funny to you, but I don't like it.

Knock, knock.

Who's there?

Doctor.

Doctor who?

No, no, just the doctor.

Knock, knock.

Who's there?

Ears.

Ears who?

Ears another knock-knock joke for you.

Knock, knock.

Who's there?

Europe.

Europe who?

Now that's just rude.

Knock, knock.

Who's there?

Gruesome.

Gruesome who?

Gruesome carrots in my garden.

Knock, knock.

Who's there?

Haven.

Haven who?

Haven you heard enough of these knock-knock jokes?

Knock, knock.

Who's there?

Hike.

Hike who?

I didn't know you liked Japanese poetry.

Knock, knock.

Who's there?

Honeybee.

Honeybee who?

Honeybee a dear and open up, will you?

Knock, knock.

Who's there?

Howl.

Howl who?

Howl you know if you don't open the door?

Knock, knock.

Who's there?

Ice cream soda.

Ice cream soda who?

Ice scream soda whole house knows I'm at the door.

Knock, knock.

Who's there?

Icing.

Icing who?

Icing so loudly so everyone can hear me.

Knock, knock.

Who's there?

Icy.

Icy who?

Icy no reason for you to keep me outside.

Knock, knock.

Who's there?

June.

June who?

June know how long I've been knocking out here?

Knock, knock.

Who's there?

Lass.

Lass who?

That's what cowboys use.

Knock, knock.

Who's there?

Moustache.

Moustache who?

Moustache you a question, but I'll shave it for later.

Knock, knock.

Who's there?

Needle.

Needle who?

Needle little help getting in the door.

Knock, knock.

Who's there?

Nuisance.

Nuisance who?

What's nuisance yesterday?

Knock, knock.

Who's there?

Nun.

Nun who?

Nun of your business.

Knock, knock.

Who's there?

Owls say.

Owls say who?

Yes, they do.

Knock, knock.

Who's there?

Unaware.

Unaware who?

Unaware is the first thing you put on in the morning.

Knock, knock.

Who's there?

Panther.

Panther who?

Panther what you can put on after your unaware.

Knock, knock.

Who's there?

Police.

Police who?

Police open the door and let me in.

Knock, knock.

Who's there?

Radio.

Radio who?

Radio not, here I come.

Knock, knock.

Who's there?

Razor.

Razor who?

Razor hand if you know the answer.

Knock, knock.

Who's there?

Repeat.

Repeat who?

Who, who, who.

Knock, knock.

Who's there?

Rita.

Rita who?

Rita lot of these jokes to your friends.

Knock, knock.

Who's there?

Santa.

Santa who?

Santa text message telling you to open the door.

Knock, knock.

Who's there?

Says.

Says who?

Says me, that's who.

Knock, knock.

Who's there?

Smell mop.

Smell mop who?

Ewww, no thanks.

Knock, knock.

Who's there?

Snow.

Snow who?

Snowbody you know, nice to meet you.

Knock, knock.

Who's there?

Spell.

Spell who?

W-H-O.

Knock, knock.

Who's there?

Stopwatch.

Stopwatch who?

Stopwatch you're doing and open the door.

Knock, knock.

Who's there?

Tank.

Tank who?

You're welcome, you're welcome.

Knock, knock.

Who's there?

Tennis.

Tennis who?

Tennis the number after nine.

Knock, knock.

Who's there?

To.

To who?

No, it's to whom.

Knock, knock.

Who's there?

Trigger.

Trigger who?

Trigger treat.

Knock, knock.

Who's there?

Voodoo.

Voodoo who?

Voodoo you think you are, asking me so many questions?

Knock, knock.

Who's there?

Waddle.

Waddle who?

Waddle you give me to stop knocking on your door?

Knock, knock.

Who's there?

Want.

Want who?

Want, who... three, four, five.

Knock, knock.

Who's there?

Water.

Water who?

Water you waiting for, open the door.

Knock, knock.

Who's there?

Wire.

Wire who?

Wire you always asking, "Who's there?"

Knock, knock.

Who's there?

Woo.

Woo who?

Don't get too excited, it's only a joke.

Knock, knock.

Who's there?

Wooden shoe.

Wooden shoe who?

Wooden shoe like to open the door now?

Knock, knock.

Who's there?

A herd.

A herd who?

A herd you were home so I came over.

Knock, knock.

Who's there?

Canoe.

Canoe who?

Canoe come out and play?

Knock, knock.

Who's there?

Al.

Al who?

Al come in if you open the door.

Knock, knock.

Who's there?

Mikey.

Mikey who?

Mikey is stuck in the lock.

Knock, knock.

Who's there?

Nadya.

Nadya who?

Nadya head if you understand.

Knock, knock.

Who's there?

Theodore.

Theodore who?

Theodore wasn't opened so I knocked.

Knock, knock.

Who's there?

Candice.

Candice who?

Candice joke get any worse?

Knock, knock.

Who's there?

Arch.

Arch who?

Bless you. Are you catching a cold?

Knock, knock.

Who's there?

Nicholas.

Nicholas who?

A Nicholas is not much money these days.

Knock, knock.

Who's there?

Watson.

Watson who?

Not much, what's new with you?

Knock, knock.

Who's there?

Doris.

Doris who?

Doris not open, that's why I'm knocking.

Knock, knock.

Who's there?

Dwayne.

Dwayne who?

Dwayne the bathtub, I'm dwowning.

Knock, knock.

Who's there?

Alex.

Alex who?

Alex-plain when you open the door.

Knock, knock.

Who's there?

Amos.

Amos who?

A mosquito.

Knock, knock.

Who's there?

Juno.

Juno who?

Juno what time it is?

Knock, knock.

Who's there?

Emma.

Emma who?

Emma gonna have to knock again, or you gonna let me in?

Knock, knock.

Who's there?

Anita.

Anita who?

Anita drink of water, I'm really thirsty.

Knock, knock.

Who's there?

Annie

Annie who?

Annie thing you can do I can better.

Knock, knock.

Who's there?

Lena.

Lena who?

Lena a little closer, and I'll tell you another joke.

Knock, knock.

Who's there?

Leon.

Leon who?

Leon me when you're not strong.

Knock, knock.

Who's there?

Stan.

Stan who?

Stan back, I'm kicking the door down.

Knock, knock.

Who's there?

Champ.

Champ who?

Champoo the dog, he was sprayed by a skunk.

Knock, knock.

Who's there?

Goat.

Goat who?

Goat to your room.

Knock, knock.

Who's there?

Dude.

Dude who?

Dude-doo in the yard, need to scoop it up.

Knock, knock.

Who's there?

Kanga.

Kanga who?

I think you mean kangaroo.

Knock, knock.

Who's there?

Zachary Oswald Turtle the Third.

Zachary Oswald Turtle the Third who?

How many Zachary Oswald Turtle the Thirds do you know?

Knock. Knock.

Who's there?

Poodle.

Poodle who?

Poodle lot of ketchup on my hot dog, please.

Knock, knock.

Who's there?

Arthur.

Arthur who?

Arthur any tasty snacks in there? I'm hungry.

Knock, knock.

Who's there?

Gorilla.

Gorilla who?

Gorilla cheese sandwich.

Knock, knock.

Who's there?

Lettuce.

Lettuce who?

Lettuce is, it's raining out here.

Knock, knock.

Who's there?

Irish stew.

Irish stew who?

Irish stew in the name of the law.

Knock, knock.

Who's there?

Pete.

Pete who?

Pete-za delivery.

Knock, knock.

Who's there?

Cabbage.

Cabbage who?

You expect a cabbage to have a last name?

Knock, knock.

Who's there?

Cash.

Cash who?

No, thanks, I'm allergic to nuts.

Knock, knock.

Who's there?

Figs.

Figs who?

Figs the doorbell.

Knock, knock.

Who's there?

Butter.

Butter who?

Butter let me in.

Knock, knock.

Who's there?

Weiner.

Weiner who?

Weiner you going to let me in?

Knock, knock.

Who's there?

Sweden.

Sweden who?

Sweden sour chicken.

Knock, knock.

Who's there?

Quiche.

Quiche who?

Can I have a hug and a quiche?

Knock, knock.

Who's there?

Orange.

Orange who?

Orange you going to let me in?

Knock, knock.

Who's there?

Turnip.

Turnip who?

Turnip the radio, that's my favourite song.

Knock, knock.

Who's there?

Avocado.

Avocado who?

Avocado cold.

Knock, knock.

Who's there?

Yoda.

Yoda who?

Yoda best.

Knock, knock.

Who's there?

Art.

Art who?

Art-2-D-2.

Knock, knock.

Who's there?

Luke.

Luke who?

Luke out - here comes another knock knock joke.

Knock, Knock.

Who's there?

Ahsoka.

Ahsoka who?

Ahsoka my dishes before I wash them.

2

Food Jokes

What has T in the beginning, T in the middle, and T at the end?

A teapot.

A fast food employee dropped my burger patty on the floor before serving it to me. They said it was ground beef.

Dan: Why don't you wanna taco 'bout it?

Sam: Because I'm nacho friend anymore.

Sam: There is a fly in my soup.

Katherine: Don't worry, the spider in your bread will get it.

Dad, will my pizza be long?

No, it will be round.

Did you hear about the fast food at the monastery?

There's a chip monk and a fish friar.

Did you hear about the new restaurant in outer space?

The food is great but there's no atmosphere.

Did you hear the joke about the peanut butter?

I'm not telling you. You might spread it.

Did you see the movie about the hot dog?

It was an Oscar Wiener.

Every morning I think I'm going to make pancakes, but I keep waffling.

Have you heard the joke about the pizza?

Never mind, it's too cheesy.

How do you get fat free milk?

From a skinny cow.

What's the easiest way to find an elephant?

Hide in a bush and make a noise like a peanut.

How do you know carrots are good for your eyes?

Have you ever seen a rabbit wearing glasses?

How do you make a milk shake?

Give it a good scare.

How do you make a sausage roll?

Push it down the hill.

How do you make a walnut laugh?

Crack it up.

How do you make an apple turnover?

Push it down the hill, too.

How fast is milk?

It's pasteurized before you know it.

Where do you learn to make ice cream?

Sundae school.

My dad hurt himself eating seafood.

He pulled a mussel.

My friend won't talk to me any more because of my obsession with pasta.

I'm feeling cannelloni right now.

My teacher bet me a hundred dollars I couldn't build a plane out of

spaghetti.

You should have seen the look on her face as I flew pasta.

Waiter, this food tastes kind of funny.

Then why aren't you laughing?

What are twins' favourite fruit?

Pears.

What can you put in a freezer that's hot but will always come

out hot?

Hot sauce.

What candy do you eat during school break?

Recess pieces.

What cheese is made backwards?

Edam.

What cheese is not yours?

Nacho cheese.

What did Bacon say to Tomato?

Lettuce get out of here.

What did one blueberry say to the other blueberry?

If you weren't so sweet, we wouldn't be in this jam.

What did the baby corn say to the mama corn?

"Where's pop corn?"

What did the banana say to its sick friend?

How are you peeling?

What did the bragging pickle say?

I'm kind of a big dill.

What did the cupcake say to the icing?

I'd be muffin without you.

What did the frog order at McDonald's?

French flies and a diet croak.

What did the frozen treat's friend say when it turned ten years old?

It's sherbert day.

What did the ghost put on his bagel?

Scream cheese.

What did the gingerbread man find on his bed?

A cookie sheet.

What did the happy slice of cheese say to the sad slice of cheese?

"It will turn out okay. Everything is gouda."

What did the hot dog say when his friend passed him in the race?

Wow, I relish the fact that you've mustard the strength to ketchup to me.

What did the hot dog bun say to the sourdough?

You're my roll model.

What did the pecan say to the walnut?

We're friends because we're both nuts.

What did the snowman order at the restaurant?

An iceberger with chili sauce.

Are you a vegetable, animal, or mineral?

Vegetable - I'm a human bean.

What did the tomato say to the other tomato?

"You go on without me, I'll ketchup."

What did the waiter say when he dropped a hotdog?

It could always be wurst.

What do elves make sandwiches with?

Shortbread

What do ghosts serve for dessert?

Ice scream and booberries.

What do race car drivers eat?

Fast food.

What do snowmen eat for breakfast?

Frosted Flakes or Ice Crispies.

My brother told me an onion is the only food that makes you cry.

So I dropped a pineapple on his foot.

What did the student say after the teacher said, "Order, students, order?"

"Can I have fries and a burger?"

Two cookies are baking in an oven. One cookie says to the other,

"Man, is it me, or is it getting kinda hot in here?"

The other cookie replies, "Oh my goodness. A talking cookie."

What is worse than finding half a worm in your apple?

Spitting the other half out.

Why did the boy throw butter out the window?

To see butter fly.

What do you call a cashew at the space station?

An astronut.

What do you call a fake noodle?

An impasta.

What do you call a mac 'n' cheese that gets all up in your face?

Too close for comfort food.

What do you call a sheep covered in chocolate?

I don't know, a Hershey baah?

What do you call a train full of bubble gum?

A chew-chew train.

What do you call an avocado that's been blessed?

Holy guacamole.

What do you call cheese that isn't yours?

Nacho cheese.

What do you call the time in between eating peaches?

A pit-stop.

What do you call three raspberries playing music?

A jam session.

What do you call two bananas?

A pair of slippers.

What do you get when a pig and a chicken bump into each other?

Ham and eggs.

What do you get when you cross a hot dog and Halloween?

A Hallo-weenie.

What do you give to a sick lemon?

Lemon aid.

What did the psychic order at McDonald's?

Medium fries.

What do you say to a sad salad?

Don't kale my vibe.

What does a nosey pepper do?

Get jalapeño business.

What does an orange do when it takes a juice test?

It concentrates.

What does it do before it rains cupcakes?

It sprinkles.

What fruit do you need if you're locked out?

A key-wi.

What happened when the strawberry was run over?

It created a traffic jam.

What happens when veggies throw a party?

They get a DJ to turnip the beet.

What has to be broken before you can use it?

An egg.

What is a math teacher's favourite dessert?

Pi.

What is a pretzel's favourite dance?

The twist.

What is a table you can eat?

A vegetable.

What is a taxi driver's favourite kind of vegetable?

A cab-bage

What is a witch's favourite food?

Ghoulash.

What happens when ice cream gets angry?

It has a melt down.

What is black; white, green and bumpy?

A pickle wearing a tuxedo.

What is green and sings?

Elvis Parsley

What is green and white when it is up and red when it hits the ground?

A watermelon.

What is green, small and round and goes up and down?

A pea in an elevator.

What is small, red and has a sore throat?

A hoarse radish.

What is the most attractive fruit?

A fine-apple.

What is white, has a horn, and gives milk?

A dairy truck.

What kind of keys do kids like to carry?

Cookies.

What kind of nut always seems to have a cold?

Cashew.

What do you get when you mix a dog with a daisy?

A collie-flower.

What kind of vegetable likes to look at animals?

A zoo-chini.

What kind of vegetable truck need when it had a flat tire?

A-spare-agus.

What type of candy is never on time?

Choco-late.

What type of vegetable looks after the elderly?

The carrot-aker.

What vegetable has eyes but can't see?

A potato.

What vegetables can't you take on a boat?

Leeks.

What's an apple's favourite compliment?

You're awesome to the core.

What's Peter Pan's favourite fast food restaurant?

Wendy's.

What's Santa's favourite candy?

Jolly Ranchers.

What's the best thing to put into a pie?

Your teeth.

What's the most emotional food at her wedding?

The wedding cake - it's always in tiers.

What's white on the inside and green on the outside?

A banana dressed up as a cucumber.

What's white, red and blue at Christmas time?

A sad candy cane.

What's a baker's favourite joke?

A cinnamon pun.

What's a ghost's favourite dessert?

Boo-berry ice scream.

What's a penguin's favourite salad ingredient?

Iceberg lettuce

What's a potato Jedi's worst enemy?

Darth Tater.

What's a tailor's favourite kind of vegetable?

A string bean.

What's a vegetable's favourite martial art?

Carrotee.

What's an egg's least favourite day of the week?

Fry-day.

What's better than a good friend?

A good friend with chocolate.

What's orange and sounds like a parrot?

A carrot.

What's the sound kids make who love their vegetables?

Brussel shouts.

When do astronauts eat?

At launch time.

When potatoes have babies, what are they called?

Tater tots.

When should you take a cookie to the doctor?

When it feels crummy.

Whenever I want to start eating healthy a chocolate bar looks at me and snickers.

Where did the spaghetti go to dance?

The meat ball.

Where do ghosts buy their food?

At the ghostery store.

Where does the Easter bunny eat breakfast?

IHOP.

Why can't eggs tell jokes?

They'd crack each other up.

Why can't you trust overloaded tacos?

Because they spill the beans.

Why wouldn't the sesame seed leave the casino?

Because he was on a roll.

Why did that kid just swallow the money his mom gave you?

He was told it was lunch money.

Why did the bacon laugh?

Because the egg cracked a yoke.

Why did the baker stop making doughnuts?

He was annoyed with the hole business.

Why did the banana go out with the prune?

Because he couldn't find a date.

Why did the banana go to the doctor?

Because it wasn't peeling well.

Why did the butcher work overtime last week?

To make ends meat.

Why did the chef have to stop cooking with herbs?

He ran out of thyme.

Why did the chicken join the band?

Because he had the drumsticks.

Why did the cookie cry?

Because his mother was a wafer too long.

Why did the cow eat the tight rope walker?

Because he wanted a balanced meal.

Why was the egg sad it was in an omelet?

It wasn't all it cracked up to be.

Why did the fisherman put peanut butter into the sea?

To go with the jellyfish.

Why did the gardener quit?

Because his celery wasn't high enough.

Why did the hamburger go to the gym?

It wanted better buns.

Why did the ice-cream truck break down?

Because of the rocky road.

Why did the jellybean go to school?

To become a smartie.

Why did the lady love to drink hot chocolate?

Because she was a cocoanut.

Why did the skeleton go to the barbecue?

To get a spare rib.

Why did the students eat their homework?

Because the teacher said that it was a piece of cake.

Why did the tofu cross the road?

To prove it wasn't chicken.

Why do melons have fancy weddings?

Because they cantaloupe.

Why do the French eat snails?

Because they don't like fast food.

Why do they only eat one egg for breakfast in France?

Because in France, one egg is an oeuf.

Why does the mushroom always get invited to parties?

Because he's a fun-gi.

Why does yogurt love going to the museum?

Because it's cultured.

Why does your dad keep candy canes locked away?

He keeps them in mint condition.

Why doesn't anyone laugh at the gardener's jokes?

Because they're too corny.

Why don't they serve chocolate in prison?

Because it makes you break out.

Why shouldn't you tell a secret on a farm?

Because the potatoes have eyes and the corn has ears.

Why was the bread dough sad?

It wanted to be kneaded by someone.

3

Nature Jokes

What bird can you buy at the grocery store?

A kiwi.

What brand of soap do birds use?

Dove.

What do you call a bunch of chickens playing hide-and-seek?

Fowl play.

What do you call a sick eagle?

Illegal.

What do you get if you cross a duck with fireworks?

A firequacker.

What do you give a sick bird?

Tweetment.

What does a bird like in his salad?

Crowtons.

What is a parrot's favourite game?

Hide and speak.

What kind of animal is a chickadee in winter?

A brrrrrd.

What kind of bird can carry the most?

The crane.

What kind of bird doesn't need a comb?

A bald eagle.

What kind of bird works at a construction site?

A crane.

What kind of bird works underground?

A mynah bird.

What kind of books do owls like?

Hoot-dunits.

What kind of math do owls like?

Owlgebra.

What's another name for a smart-alecky duck?

A wise quacker.

When do teachers carry crackers?

On parrot-teacher conference days.

When should you buy a bird?

When it's goes cheep.

Where do birds invest their money?

In the stork market.

Which bird is out of breath all the time?

A puffin.

Why did the bird want to join the army?

He wanted to be a parrot trooper.

Why did the pelican bring a lot of money to the restaurant?

Because he had a very big bill.

Why do crows sit on telephone poles?

To make long distance caws.

Why do I hear the song "You Need To Calm Down" coming from my fireplace?

You have a Taylor chimney swift.

Why does a flamingo lift up one leg?

Because if it lifted both legs it would fall over.

Why would you call the police get rid of bugs?

Because they have a S.W.A.T. team.

How do bees brush their hair?

With a honey comb.

How do bees get to school?

They take the buzz.

What do you say to start a firefly race?

Ready. Set. Glow.

How do fleas travel?

They itch-hike.

What did old caterpillars use to order Christmas gifts?

Cater-logs.

What did one girl firefly say to the other girl firefly?

You glow, girl.

What did the sushi roll say to the bee?

Wassabee.

What do ants use to smell better?

Deodor-ant.

What do bees say when they get back to their hive?

"Honey, I'm back."

What do fireflies eat?

Light snacks.

What do moths study in school?

Mothematics.

What do you call a bee's bum?

It's bee-hind.

What do you call a beetle that can dance?

A jitterbug.

What do you call a bug that can't have too much sugar?

A diabeetle.

What do you call a bug that jumps inside your cupboard?

A glasshopper.

What do you call a cricket that takes pictures?

A shutterbug.

What do you call a funny chicken?

A comedi-hen

What do you call a really old ant?

An antique.

What do you call a wasp?

A wanna-bee.

What do you call two spiders who just got married?

Newlywebs.

What do you do with a sick wasp?

Take it to the waspital.

What do you get when you cross an insect and a rabbit?

Bugs Bunny.

What insect are you most likely to find in school?

A spelling bee.

What is a bug's favourite sport?

Cricket.

What is a caterpillar scared of?

A dog-erpillar.

What is a mosquito's favourite sport?

Skin diving.

What is worse than finding half a worm in your apple?

Spitting the other half out.

What kind of bugs live in clocks?

Ticks.

What kind of car do bugs like to drive?

A Volkswagen Beetle.

What was the best bug band ever?

The Beatles.

What was the spider doing on the computer?

Searching the web.

What's a caterpillar's favourite weapon?

A cater-polt.

When do spiders go on their honeymoon?

After their webbing day.

Where do ants go for winter vacation?

Antarctica.

Where's the best place to buy bugs?

A flea market.

Why are spiders good at computer safety?

They catch bugs on the web.

Why did the boy throw butter out the window?

To see butter fly.

Why did the fly fly?

Because the spider spied her.

Why didn't the butterfly want to go to the dance?

Because she heard it was a moth ball.

Why do humming birds hum?

Because they can't remember the words.

Why don't people like bed bugs?

Because they get under their skin.

Why is the centipede always late for school?

Well, just think of all the shoes it has to put on.

Why was the fly looking for the garbage can?

Because he was a litterbug.

Why was the grocery store out of butter?

Because butter flies.

Did you know I can cut a tree down by looking at it?

It's true. I saw it with my own eyes.

Do you want a brief explanation of an acorn?

In a nutshell, it's an oak tree.

How did the dummy get hurt while raking leaves?

He fell out of the tree.

How do trees access the internet?

They log on.

How do trees resolve arguments?

They sign a tree-ty.

How do you identify a dogwood tree?

By its bark.

How was the acorn feeling after it was buried?

It was feeling oak-ay.

I asked my dad, "Would you ever go on all-cashew diet?"

He said, "No, that's just nuts."

What did the Jedi knight say to the sacred tree?

May the forest be with you.

66

What did the tree do when the bank closed?

It started its own branch.

What did the trees wear to the pool party?

Swimming trunks.

What do you get when you cross a cat with a lemon tree?

A sour puss.

What do you give to a sick citrus tree?

Lemon aid.

What gets a year older whenever it rings?

A tree.

What happens to the romantic trees every Valentine's Day?

They get sappy.

What is a tree's favourite part of math?

Treegonometree.

What is a tree's least favourite month?

Sep-timberrrr.

What is a tree's favourite shape?

A treeangle.

What is the same shape as a tall pine tree but weighs nothing?

The shadow of a tall pine tree.

What kind of a tree do science teachers plant?

Chemist-tree.

What kind of flowers will grow when you plant kisses?

Tulips.

What kind of tree grows chickens?

Poultree.

What kind of tree fits right in your hand?

A palm tree.

What weighs more: a pound of leaves or a pound of logs?

They both weigh exactly the same amount.

Did you hear the famous noisy bird walking through the leaves?

It was Rustle Crow.

When are trees less stressed out?

In spring, when they are releaved.

Where do young trees go to learn?

Elementree school.

Which tree radio station plays all today's hits?

Poplar FM.

Which trees miss the most school days because of colds and flu?

The sycamore.

Why do you say leaves are risk-takers?

They are always out on a limb, that's why.

Which tree has the most friends?

The poplar one.

Why did a bunch of trees all take a nap at the same time?

For rest.

Why was the pine tree in a bad mood at Christmas?

Because it was on Santa's knotty list.

Why do dogwood trees make good pets?

They have a nice bark, but they wooden bite.

Why do trees hate lumberjack tests?

Because they get stumped.

Why do trees make the worst enemies?

Because they are really good at throwing shade.

Which city do trees go to when they want to watch a hockey game?

Montreeal.

4

Pet Jokes

Do bunnies use combs?

No, they use hare brushes.

Do you want to hear a bad cat joke?

Just kitten.

How did the bird break into the house?

With a crow bar.

How do rabbits get from one garden to another?

They take a taxi cabbage.

How do dog catchers get paid?

By the pound.

How do fleas travel from place to place?

By itch-hiking.

How do you know carrots are good for your eyes?

Because you never see a rabbit wearing glasses.

How do you stop a dog from barking in your front yard?

Put him in your backyard.

How does a dog stop a TV show to get a snack?

She presses the paws button.

How does a mouse feel after it takes a shower?

Squeaky clean.

How is cat food sold?

Usually purr can.

How is your cat doing?

She is feline fine.

How many hairs in a rabbit's tail?

None - they are all on the outside.

I asked my dog for a joke about the top of our house.

She said, "Roof roof".

What did the Dalmatian say after his meal?

"That hit the spots."

There were ten cats in a boat and one jumped out. How many were left?

None, because they were all copycats.

What airline do rabbits use?

Hare Canada.

What bird do you always see at lunchtime?

A swallow.

What kind of dog makes the best watch dog?

A clocker spaniel.

What did one flea say to the other?

Should we walk or take a dog?

What did the cowboy say when his puppy was missing?

"Well, doggone."

What did the dog say to the flea?

Quit bugging me.

What did the dog say to the tree?

Bark.

What did the dog think when he sat on sandpaper?

Rough, rough.

What did the fish say when he got out of jail?

"I'm off the hook."

What did the rabbit give his girlfriend?

A 14 carrot ring.

What do bunnies sing at birthday parties?

Hoppy birthday to you.

What do cats like to eat on sunny days?

Mice cream cones.

Where do cats like to look at for shopping ideas?

Cat-alogues.

What do cats wear at night?

Paw-jamas.

What do fish need to stay healthy?

Vitamin sea.

What do you call a bunny that has fleas?

Bugs Bunny.

What do you call a bunny transformer?

Hop-timus Prime.

What do you call a cat on ice?

One cool cat.

What do you call a cat that can handle a catastrophe?

A survival kit.

What do you call a cat that does tricks?

A magic kit.

What do you call a cat that gets anything it wants?

Purrr-suasive.

What's the secret to good-smelling cats?

Purrrr-fume.

What do you call a dog with a Timex?

A watch dog.

What do you call a frozen dog?

A pupsicle.

What do you call a great dog detective?

Sherlock Bones.

What do you call a kitten that likes to cuddle?

Paws-itively purrrfect.

What do you call a large dog that pays attention to her surroundings?

Aware wolf.

What do you call a newbie hamster?

Hamateur.

What is the rudest bird in the world?

A mockingbird.

What do you call an operation on a rabbit?

A hare-cut.

What do you call it when a cat wins a dog show?

A cat-has-trophy.

What do you do if you catch your dog eating your dictionary?

You take the words right out of his mouth.

What do you get if you cross a gold dog with a telephone?

A golden receiver.

What do you get when you cross a frog and a dog?

A croaker spaniel.

What do you get when you cross a parrot and a centipede?

A walkie-talkie.

What do you get when you cross a rabbit with a leaf blower?

A hare dryer.

What do you get when you pour hot water into a cranky rabbit's home?

A hot cross bunny.

What do you give a dog who behaves really well?

A bone-us.

What do birds say at Halloween?

Trick or tweet.

What does a bird like in his soup?

Crowtons.

What does my dog and my phone have in common?

They both have collar I.D.

What dog can jump higher than a tree?

Any dog can jump higher than a tree, trees can't jump.

What happened when a hundred hares escaped from the school's rabbit farm?

The teachers had to comb the area.

What happened when the dog went to the flea circus?

He stole the show.

What has fur and whiskers and cuts grass?

A lawn meower.

What is a dog's favourite food?

Anything that is on your plate.

What is a mouse's favourite game?

Hide and squeak.

What is small, squeaky, and great at sword fights?

A mouseketeer.

What kind of cats like to go bowling?

Alley cats.

What kind of dog does Dracula have?

A bloodhound.

What kind of dog keeps the best time?

A watch dog.

What kind of pet is the least expensive?

The budgie - it's cheep cheep.

What month do dogs bark the least?

February - it is the shortest month.

What side of a cat has more fur?

The outside.

What type of market should you never take your dog?

A flea market.

What's a dog's favourite kind of pizza?

Pupperoni pizza.

What's a dog's ideal research job?

Barkeologist.

What's grey, squeaky and hangs around in caves?

Stalagmice.

What's the best way to catch a fish?

Have someone throw it to you gently.

Where does a hamster go for Spring Break?

Hamsterdam.

Which breed of dog is the quietest?

A hush puppy.

Which dog breed is guaranteed to laugh at all of your jokes?

A Chi-ha-ha.

Who do fish always know how much they weigh?

Because they have their own scales.

Why are cats so good at video games?

Because they have nine lives.

Why aren't dogs good dancers?

Because they have two left feet.

Why did the cat cross the road?

It was the chicken's day off.

Why did the cat put the letter "M" into the fridge?

Because it turns "ice" into "mice".

Why did the Dalmatian go to the eye doctor?

He kept seeing spots.

Why did the dog cross the road twice?

He was trying to fetch a boomerang.

Why do dogs wag their tails?

Because no one else will do it for them.

Why is a tree like a noisy dog?

They both have a lot of bark.

Why is it against the law to let an eagle get sick?

Because then it is illegal.

Why was the mouse afraid of the water?

He saw a catfish.

Why did the doctor have a Labrador retriever and kitten at work?

In case she needed to do a cat scan or get a lab report.

Knock, knock.

Who's there?

Dude.

Dude who?

Dude-doo in the yard, need to scoop it up.

What's the difference between a strange rabbit and a strong rabbit?

One is a bit funny, and the other is a fit bunny.

Did you ever see a fish bowl?

Yes.

Did she get a strike or a spare?

How did the Scottish dog feel when he saw the Loch Ness monster?

Terrier-fied.

The more the rabbit takes away from it, the bigger it becomes. What is it?

A rabbit hole.

"All hundred sheep are in now," the talking sheepdog told the farmer.

"But I only have ninety-five sheep," says the farmer.

"I know," replies the sheepdog. "But I rounded them up."

My friend and I both have cats. My cat's name is One Two Three, and her cat's name is Un Deux Trois. Our cats raced across the pond - guess who won?

One Two Three won, because Un Deux Trois cat sank.

5

Random Funny Jokes

What is a robot's favourite snack?

Computer chips.

What do you call spughetti?

An impasta.

What jam can't be eaten on toast?

A traffic jam.

What kind of key opens a banana?

A monkey.

Where do cannibals eat when they are on a car trip?

Wherever they serve truck drivers.

Why did the cannibal spit out the clown?

Because he tasted funny.

The cannibal child was too late for supper.

His dad said, "Sorry, everyone's already eaten."

Which bean do kids like best?

The jellybean.

What cake do you use when you want to clean your plate?

A sponge cake.

The nervous sword swallower went on a diet.

He was on pins and needles for months.

What kind of berry would you use with a colouring book?

A crayon-berry.

What did the nut say when it got a cold?

Cashew.

Why did the man stop working at the orange juice shop?

He couldn't concentrate.

Did you hear the rumour about butter?

I'll tell you if you promise not to spread it.

What did the hamburger name his daughter?

Patty.

Did you hear about the race between the lettuce and the tomato?

The lettuce was a head, but the tomato was trying to ketchup.

Why did the woman start a pizza shop?

She wanted to make some dough.

I was so hungry at seven fifty-nine that I eight o'clock.

Let minnow if you can think of a good fish pun.

Why did the guy take a bath in vegetable oil?
He wanted to wake up oily in the morning.

Why did the baby strawberry cry?
Because his family was in a jam.

What the favorite fruit of twins?
Pears.

What do you call a pea who didn't get enough sleep?
Grum-pea.

What's the hottest letter in the alphabet?
B. You add it to oil and it makes it boil.

What is the longest word in the dictionary?
Smiles starts with an s, ends with an s, with a mile in between.

Did you know there used to be only 25 letters in the alphabet?

Nobody knew why.

What starts with a p, ends with an e, and has a million letters in it?

Post office.

What race is never run?

A swimming race.

What has four wheels and flies?

A garbage truck.

What is the tallest building in the world?

The library. It has the most stories.

What has three letters and starts with gas?

A car.

Did you know each day starts with destruction?

The day breaks at the crack of dawn.

What has many teeth but cannot chew?

A comb.

Why won't a bicycle stand up when it's not moving?

It's too tired.

Why can't your nose be 12 inches long?

If it was 12 inches long, then it would be a foot.

What is the center of gravity?

The letter V.

How do you make a pirate angry?

Take away the p.

What is the most magical dog?

A labracadabrador.

Which dinosaur gets into car accidents?

Tyrannosaurus wrecks.

What sound do porcupines make when they kiss?

Ouch.

What do you call a dinosaur when it's asleep?

A dino-snore.

What goes meow-meow-meow-meow-meow-meow-meow-meow in the ocean?

An octo-puss.

What is the biggest ant in the world?

An eleph-ant.

What do you call a sleeping bull?

A bulldozer.

What kind of bird hangs out with a bulldozer?

A crane.

Why do seagulls only fly over the sea?

If they went across the bay, then they would be bagels.

Why do birds fly south for the winter?

It is easier than walking.

Where do sheep get haircuts?

At the baa-baa shop.

What's the most musical pet?

A trum-pet.

Did you hear that 1,000 hares escaped from the rabbit farm?

Police are combing the area.

How do you make a skunk stop smelling?

Give it nose plugs.

Why are some fish at the bottom of the ocean?

Because they dropped out of school.

What did the buffalo say to his boy when he dropped him off at school?

Bison.

Why do bees have such sticky hair?

Because they love their honeycomb.

How do you make an octopus laugh?

With ten-tickles.

What bug is welcome in apartments?

Ten-ants.

Why do tigers have stripes?

So they don't get spotted.

Where do young cows eat at school?

At the calf-eteria.

What do you call bears with no ears?

B.

What is a bunny's motto?

Don't worry, be hoppy.

How do rabbits travel?

By hareplane.

How much space do fungi need to grow?

As mushroom as possible.

How do trees get on the internet?

They log on.

What did the dentist get for an award?

A little plaque.

When time do most people remember to go to the dentist?

Tooth-hurty.

Why did you handcuff the piano player's hands behind his back?

To see if he could play by ear.

Why did the gardener bury her wallet in the ground?

She wanted the soil to be rich.

What amazing luck! A writer dropped five stories into a garbage can and walked away unhurt.

Which month do soldiers hate most?

The month of March.

Why did the robber take a bath?

He wanted to make a clean getaway.

When do doctors get cranky?

When they run out of patients.

Why did the person quit their job as an origami teacher?

Too much paperwork.

What is a pirate's favourite letter?

Arrrrr.

Why did the pirate pay two dollars to get his ears pierced?

He was a buck an ear.

Why couldn't the pirate play cards?

Because he was sitting on the deck.

Why couldn't the ten-year-old go see the pirate movie?

Because it was rated arrrrr.

What did the pirate say on his 80th birthday?

Aye Matey!

How did the barber win the race?

With a short cut.

What sport are hairdressers great at?

Curling.

What's an astronaut's favourite candy?

A Mars bar.

Where do astronauts leave their spaceships?

At parking meteors.

How do you make an astronaut's baby fall asleep?
You rocket.

How do astronauts serve dinner in outer space?
On flying saucers.

What kind of music do astronauts listen to?
Neptunes.

How does a scientist freshen her breath?
With experi-mints.

What kind of flower creates electricity?
A power plant.

Do you have dead batteries to give away?
Yes, they are free of charge.

What kitchen appliance washes up on very small beaches?
Microwaves.

Did you hear about the piece of wood that was grounded?

It was bored.

Why is 6 afraid of 7?

Because 7 ate 9.

Why did 7 eat 9?

He wanted to have 3 squared meals a day.

The police are chasing the hacker.

Witnesses said he went data way.

I asked my librarian where I could find books on electricity.

She asked, "Current events or light reading?"

Where does bad light go?

Prism.

What did the volcano say to her husband?

I lava you so much.

Which kind of scientist should get more sun?

A paleontologist.

Did you hear thunder and lightning in the school science lab?

The students were brainstorming.

Why can you never trust atoms?

They make up everything.

Where are the smartest trees found?

In the brainforest.

What will go viral no many how popular it gets?

Antibiotics.

Why did the cloud date the fog?

He was so down to earth.

What does a cloud wear under his pants?

Thunderwear.

Where do geologists sit to relax?

In a rocking chair.

What's a math teacher's favorite tree?

Geometry.

Why did the scientist read the book on helium in one night?

She couldn't put it down.

How do you throw a party in space?

You planet.

Why did the scientists take out their doorbells?

They wanted to win the no-bell prize.

6

Halloween Jokes

What does a skeleton say before serving supper?

Bone appétit.

What is a vampire's favourite fruit?

A neck-tarine.

What do Italians eat on Halloween?

Fettuccine afraido.

What is a monster's favourite food?

Ghoul Guide cookies.

What kind of hot dog do you eat on Halloween?

A Halloweenie.

What does a vampire never order at a restaurant?

A stake sandwich.

What do you get when you're stuck between two witches at the beach?

Sandwitched.

What is a vampire's favourite ice cream flavour?

Vein-illa.

What do ghosts use to wash their hair?

Sham-boo.

Why are ghosts so bad at lying?

Because you can see right through them.

Why do ghosts make good cheerleaders?

Because they have a lot of spirit.

What is a ghost's favourite fruit?

Boo-berries.

Where do ghosts buy their food?

At the ghost-ery store.

What do ghosts drink when they're thirsty on Halloween?

Ghoul-aid.

What does the papa ghost say to his family when he's driving?

Fasten your sheet belts.

What do ghosts say when something is really neat?

Ghoul.

What happens when a ghost gets lost in the fog?

He is mist.

What is a ghost's favourite way to travel?

By scareplane.

What tops off a ghost's ice cream sundae?

Whipped scream.

What kind of makeup do ghosts wear?

Mas-scare-a.

Where do ghosts mail their letters?

At the ghost office.

What are a ghost's favourite rides at the carnival?

The roller ghoster and the scary-go-round.

Who was the most famous ghost detective?

Sherlock Moans.

What kind of gum do ghosts chew?

Boo-boo Gum.

What kind of tie does a ghost wear to a formal party?

A boo-tie.

What's a ghost's favourite dessert?

Boo-berry pie and ice scream.

When does a ghost have breakfast?

In the moaning.

What is a ghost's favourite party game?

Hide-and-go-shriek.

What kind of roads do ghosts haunt?

Dead ends.

What do ghosts drink at breakfast?

Coffee with scream and sugar.

Why do ghosts like to ride elevators?

It raises their spirits.

Where do baby ghosts go during the day?

Day-scare centres.

What is in a ghost's nose?

Boo-gers.

What did the boy ghost say to the girl ghost?

You are the most booooooooo-tiful thing I have ever seen.

What kind of shoes does a ghost wear?

Boooooooooots.

What type of trees do ghosts like most?

Ceme-trees.

What did the ghost bring his ghost girlfriend?

A boo-quet.

What kind of mistakes do ghosts make?

Boo-boos.

Where do fashionable ghosts shop for sheets?

Boo-tiques.

Who are the werewolves' cousins?

The whowolves , the whatwolves, and the whenwolves.

Where do most werewolves live?

In Howl-lywood, California

What do you call a giant pumpkin?

A plumpkin.

Why does a cemetery have to keep a fence around it?

Because people are dying to get in.

Who did Frankenstein take to the dance?

His ghoulfriend.

Why is Superman's costume so tight?

Because he wears a size "S".

When is it bad luck to be followed by a black cat?

When you're a mouse.

What did one owl say to the other owl?

Happy Owl-ween.

Where did the goblin throw the football?

Over the ghoul line.

Who is the messiest monster at suppertime?

The goblin.

What do you get when you cross a black cat with a lemon?

A sour-puss.

Why was the computer scary?

It had a terrorbyte.

How do monsters tell their future?

They read their horrorscope.

Why did the horseman from Sleepy Hollow go to business school?

He wanted to get a head in life.

What do sea monsters eat for lunch?

Fish and ships.

I want to be something really scary for Halloween
this year so I'm dressing up as an iPad with 2%
battery.

What do you do when zombies surround your house?

Hope it's Halloween.

What do vegan zombies eat?

GRAAAAAAAAINS.

Do zombies eat popcorn with their fingers?

No, they eat the fingers separately.

What did the zombie give to his girlfriend for her
birthday?

Precious tombstone jewelry.

Why do you win the Halloween contest every year
with your sandwich costume?

I'm on a roll.

The maker of this product does not want it, the buyer does not use it, and the user does not see it. What is it?

A coffin.

Knock, knock.

Who's there?

Annie.

Annie who?

Annie body home?

Knock, knock.

Who's there?

Ben.

Ben who?

Ben waiting for Halloween all year.

What is a mummy's favourite type of music?

Wrap.

Why was the mummy so tense?

Because it was all wound up.

Why do mummies have so much trouble keeping friends?

They're too wrapped up in themselves.

What do you call a mummy who eats cookies in bed?

A crummy mummy.

Why don't mummies take vacations?

They're afraid they'll relax and unwind.

Why can you trust a mummy with your secret?

They can keep anything under wraps.

Why didn't the skeleton want to go to school?

His heart wasn't in it.

Why didn't the skeleton cross the road?

He didn't have any guts.

Why did the other skeleton cross the road?

To get to the body shop.

Why is a skeleton so mean?

He doesn't have a heart.

Why don't skeletons ever feel insulted?

Because nothing gets under their skin.

When does a skeleton laugh?

When something tickles his funny bone

Who was the most famous skeleton detective?

Sherlock Bones.

What do you give a skeleton for valentine's day?

Bone-bones in a heart-shaped box.

Why did the skeleton stay out in the snow all night?

He was a numb skull.

Why did the skeleton go to a BBQ?

For the spare ribs.

Why was the skeleton a bad archer?

Someone stole his bone and marrow.

Why did the skeleton go disco dancing?

To see the boogie man.

Why was the boy afraid of a skeleton?

Because it had a bone to pick with him.

How does a skeleton open his front door?

With a skeleton key.

What musical instrument does a skeleton play?

Trom-bone.

Why didn't the skeleton go to the Halloween party?

Because he had no body to go with.

What do you call a skeleton that is always sleeping?

Lazy bones.

How do skeletons travel in an emergency?

In a skele-copter.

What instruments don't you see in a skeleton band?

Organs.

Why did the skeleton love its ceramics class?

He loved making skullptures.

What do you call a stupid skeleton?

A bonehead.

What is the skeleton's funniest bone?

Humerus.

What do skeletons use to text each other?

A cell-bone.

Where do vampires keep their money?

The blood bank.

Why did the vampire need mouthwash?

Because he had bat breath.

What do vampires take when they are sick?

Coffin drops.

What do you get when you cross a duck with a vampire?

Count Quackula.

What do you get when you cross a snowman with a vampire?

Frostbite.

Where does Count Dracula usually eat his lunch?

At the casketeria.

Why didn't the vampire bite Taylor Swift?

Because she had bad blood.

How many vampires are in this room?

I don't know, I can't Count Draculas.

What is a vampire's favourite holiday?

Fangs-giving.

What happened when the two vampires finally met?

It was love at first bite.

Which building does Dracula visit in New York?

The Vampire State Building.

What do you call a vampire without a girlfriend?

A bat-chelor

What's it called when a vampire has trouble with his house?

A grave problem.

What is a vampire's least favourite food?

Stake.

How can you tell a vampire likes baseball?

Every night he turns into a bat.

What songs does Dracula hate?

"You Are My Sunshine" and "Sunshine on my Shoulder".

Why doesn't anybody like Dracula?

He has a bat temper.

What has webbed feet, feathers, fangs and goes quack-quack?

Count Duckula.

Why are vampires like dentures?

They all come out at night.

Who does Dracula get letters from?

His fang club.

Why did Dracula take cold medicine?

To stop his coffin.

What type of dog does every vampire have?

Bloodhound.

What is a vampire's favourite sport?

Casketball.

What did you say when you knocked out Dracula in a feather pillow fight?

Down for the count.

Which sports do vampires love to play?

Bat-minton.

What is the most important subject a witch learns in school?

Spelling.

What does a witch use to keep her hair up?

Scare-spray.

What do you call a witch's garage?

A broom closet.

What do you get when there's a witch in the desert?

You get a sandwich.

What do witches get at hotels?

Broom service.

What does a witch do on her birthday?

She spell-abrates.

Why don't angry witches ride their brooms?

They're afraid of flying off the handle.

What did the little witch want for her birthday?

A haunted doll house.

How do you make a witch itch?

Take away the W.

What do you get when a witch spins around a bunch of times?

A dizzy spell.

Why does a witch ride a broom?

Vacuum cleaners get stuck at the end of the cord.

What do you call two witches living together?

Broommates.

What happens if you see twin witches?

You won't be able to see which witch is which.

Why did the witch give up fortune telling?

There was no future in it.

What is a witch with poison ivy called?

An itchy witchy.

What's a cold, evil candle called?

The wicked wick of the north.

Why do all the witches like to wander on brooms?

Because the vacuum cleaners are too expensive for them.

How does a witch tell time?

She looks at her witch watch.

Who turns off the lights on Halloween?

The lights witch.

7

Christmas Jokes

What is a snowman's favourite breakfast?

Frosted Flakes.

What never eats at Christmas?

The turkey - it's stuffed.

What is the crankiest winter food?

A brrrrr-grrrrr.

What does a snowman call a block of snow?

An ice crispie square.

Why did the turkey cross the road?

Because he wasn't chicken.

What do snowmen eat for lunch at the North Pole?

Icebergers.

Elves make sandwiches with what kind of bread?

Shortbread.

What's the best thing to put into a Christmas cookie?

Your teeth.

What did the gingerbread man put under his blankets?

A cookie sheet.

How do salt, pepper, nutmeg, cinnamon, and mint sign their Christmas cards?

Seasons greetings.

Why was the turkey asked to join the North Pole Band?

Because he had the drum sticks.

Who says "Oh! Oh! Oh!"

Santa walking backwards.

Who delivers presents to baby sharks at Christmas?

Santa Jaws.

Why did Santa put a clock in his sleigh?

He wanted to see time fly.

What happens to Santa get if he's stuck in a chimney?

He gets claustrophobic.

Why does Santa have three gardens?

So he can ho, ho, ho.

What is the name of Santa's dog?

Santa Paws.

Where does Santa stay on vacation?

At the ho-ho-hotel.

How do you know Santa is good at jiu-jitsu?

Because he has a black belt.

How much did Santa pay for his sleigh?

Nothing - it was on the house.

How did Santa Claus open the front door?

He used a tur-key

What does Santa use in his washing machine?

Yule-Tide.

What do the elves call it when their boss claps his hands?

Santapplause.

What do you call a creature that's half-horse, half-Santa?

A santaur.

What do they use at the North Pole to kill germs?

Santa-tizer.

What happens to elves when they behave naughty?

Santa gives them the sack.

What kind of music do elves listen to?

Wrap.

What can you say about a greedy elf?

He's elfish.

What's the first thing Santa's helpers learn at school?

The elfabet.

What kind of cars do elves drive?

Toy-otas.

What do you call an elf who steals gift wrapping paper from the rich and gives it to the poor?

Ribbon Hood

What units of measurement do elves use in the workshop?

Santameters.

How do the elves capture memories at the workshop?

They take elfies using North Pole-aroids.

The elves use solar and wind power in the workshop.

You could say it's elf-sufficient.

Why did the elf push his bed into the fireplace?

He wanted to sleep like a log.

Eleven elves already in the workshop. What do you call the next elf to join?

The twelf.

How do elves get to the top floor of Santa's workshop?

They use the elf-evator.

What do the elves cook with in the kitchen?

Utinsel.

How does an elf get to Santa's workshop?

By icicle.

Which of Santa's reindeer has bad manners?

Rude-olph.

Did you know Rudolph never went to school?

He was elf-taught.

Why did Santa only have eight reindeer?

Comet stayed home to clean the sink.

What's the difference between Santa's reindeer and a knight?

One is dragging the sleigh, the other is slaying the dragon.

What does a reindeer say before telling you a joke?

This one is going to sleigh you.

How does Rudolph know when Christmas is coming?

He refers to his calen-deer.

If a reindeer lost his tail, where would it go for a new one?

A re-tail shop.

Which reindeer have the shortest legs?

The smallest ones.

How do you make a slow reindeer fast?

You don't feed it.

What do reindeer have that no other animals have?

Baby reindeer.

Which reindeer should you ask to the snow ball?

Dancer.

What do reindeer use when they go fishing?

Their ant-lures.

How do you get into Rudolph's house?

You ring the deer-bell.

Where do the reindeer like to stop for lunch?

Deery Queen.

How do reindeers sign cards to their cousins?

Merry Christmoose.

What has a jolly laugh, brings your presents and scratches up your furniture?

Santa Claws.

What do reindeer hang on their Christmas trees?

Horn-aments.

Knock, knock.

Who's there?

Holly

Holly who?

Holly-days are here again.

Why did Scrooge keep a pet lamb?

Because it would say, "Baaaaahh humbug!"

Why is it always cold at Christmas?

Because it's in Decembrrrrrr.

What can you get if you eat Christmas decorations?

Tinselitus.

What do you get when you cross an apple with a Christmas tree?

A pineapple.

What do you get when Santa Claus investigates missing toys?

Santa Clues.

Knock-knock.

Who's there?

Olive.

Olive who?

Olive the other reindeer.

What did the cow say on Christmas morning?

Mooooey Christmas

What happens if your rocket stalls on Christmas Eve?

You get a mistletoe.

Knock-knock.

Who's there?

Mary.

Mary who?

Mary Christmas.

When is a boat just like snow?

When its adrift.

Knock-knock.

Who's there?

Snow.

Snow who?

Snow use - I've forgotten my name.

What does December have that no other month has?

The letter D.

What type of pine has the sharpest needles?

A porcupine.

What do you call a chicken at the North Pole?

Lost.

How do cats greet each other at Christmas?

Have a Furry Merry Christmas and a Happy Mew Year!

What is a skunk's favourite song?

Jingle Smells.

What is a librarian's favourite song for library nights?

Silent Night.

What dog is mentioned in Jingle Bells?

Daschund through the snow.

What is whip cream's favourite Christmas song?

"We Whisk You A Merry Christmas."

Knock-knock.

Who's there?

Hannah.

Hannah who.

Hannah a partridge in a pear tree.

Knock-knock.

Who's there?

Murray.

Murray who?

Murray Christmas.

Knock-knock.

Who's there?

Pizza.

Pizza who?

Pizza on earth and good will toward men.

Knock-knock.

Who's there.

Dexter.

Dexter who?

Dexter halls with boughs of holly.

Why are Christmas trees so bad at sewing?

They always drop their needles.

What happened to the thief who stole an Advent calendar?

He got twenty-five days.

What do you call a frog hanging from the ceiling?

Mistletoad.

Where does mistletoe go to become famous?

Holly wood.

Who is a Christmas tree's favourite singer?

Spruce Springsteen.

What's the best Christmas present?

You can't beat a broken drum.

Why is Darth Vader tough to surprise on Christmas?

Because he can sense your presents.

I asked for a Star Wars car.

They gave me a toy Yoda.

One Christmas I got a pack of batteries with a note saying, "Toy not included."

How many presents can Santa fit in an empty sack?

Only one – after that it's not empty any more.

Why was the snowman rooting in the bag of carrots?

He was picking his nose.

What do you call Frosty the Snowman in summer?

A puddle.

Where does Frosty keep his money?

In the snow bank.

Why does everybody like Frosty the Snowman?

Because he is cool.

What does Frosty like the most about school?

Snow and tell.

What does Frosty think about?

Snow idea.

Where does Frosty and his girlfriend go to dance?

The snowball.

How do you know that a snowman is not in a good mood?

When he gives you the cold shoulder.

What's a snowman's favourite Mexican food?

Brrrrrr-itos.

What song do you sing at a snowman's birthday party?

Freeze a jolly good fellow!

Who helps you lift your car when you get a flat tire during winter?

Jack Frost.

8

More Knock Knock Jokes

Knock, knock.

Who's there?

Dwayne.

Dwayne who.

Dwayne the Knock Johnson.

Knock, knock.

Who's there?

Tish.

Tish who?

Yes, thank you, I need to blow my nose.

Knock, knock.

Who's there?

Sadie.

Sadie who?

Sadie magic words and I'll tell you.

Knock, knock.

Who's there?

Horton hears a.

Horton hears a who?

Hey, I like that Dr. Seuss book, too.

Knock, knock.

Who's there?

Rufus.

Rufus who?

Rufus leaking and I'm getting wet.

Knock, knock.

Who's there?

Ada.

Ada who?

Ada lot for breakfast and now I feel full.

Knock, knock.

Who's there?

Hugo.

Hugo who?

Hugo your way, and I'll go mine.

Knock, knock.

Who's there?

Colleen.

Colleen who?

Colleen up your room, it's a mess.

Knock, knock.

Who's there?

Chuck.

Chuck who?

I'm here to chuck wood, don't ask me how much.

Knock, knock.

Who's there?

Allison.

Allison who?

Allison to my music all day long.

Knock, knock.

Who's there?

Pete.

Pete who?

Pete-za delivery.

Knock, knock.

Who's there?

Norma Lee.

Norma Lee who?

Norma Lee I have my keys with me to open this door.

Knock, knock.

Who's there?

Hugh.

Hugh who?

Hugh can't fool me, I'm not telling.

Knock, knock.

Who's there?

Fiona.

Fiona who?

Fiona of the house is in, I'd like to speak with him.

Knock, knock.

Who's there?

Duncan.

Duncan who?

Duncan your chickens before they hatch.

Knock, knock.

Who's there?

Mary Lee.

Mary Lee who?

Mary Lee, Mary Lee, life is but a dream. Row, Row, row your boat.

Knock, knock.

Who's there?

Ringo.

Ringo who?

Ringo round the roses.

Knock, knock.

Who's there?

Al.

Al who?

Al give you a surprise if you open this door.

Knock, knock.

Who's there?

Champ.

Champ who?

Shampoo your hair to make it soft and shiny.

Knock, knock.

Who's there?

Theodore.

Theodore who?

Theodore is stuck, please help me open it.

Knock, knock.

Who's there?

Les.

Les who?

Les go out for a picnic.

Knock, knock.

Who's there?

Sid.

Sid who?

Sid down. It's time to eat.

Knock, knock.

Who's there?

Philip.

Philip who?

Philip my gas tank, please, I've got a long way to go.

Knock, knock.

Who's there?

Rena.

Rena who?

Rena this bell doesn't seem to do any good.

Knock, knock.

Who's there?

Rita.

Rita who?

Rita book from the library every week and you'll get smart.

Knock, knock.

Who's there?

Henrietta.

Henrietta who?

Henrietta worm that was in his apple.

Knock, knock.

Who's there?

Wayne.

Wayne who?

Wayne, Wayne, go away, come again another day.

Knock, knock.

Who's there?

Isadore.

Isadore who?

Is the doorbell ringing?

Knock, knock.

Who's there?

Broccoli

Broccoli who?

Broccoli doesn't have a last name, silly.

Knock, knock.

Who's there?

Cereal.

Cereal who?

Cereal pleasure to meet you.

Knock, knock.

Who's there?

Butter.

Butter who?

Butter let me in, it's raining out here.

Knock, knock.

Who's there?

Peas.

Peas who?

Peas to meet you.

Knock, knock.

Who's there?

Ice cream soda.

Ice cream soda who?

Ice scream soda whole world can hear me.

Knock, knock.

Who's there?

Water.

Water who?

Water you waiting for, please open the door.

Knock, knock.

Who's there?

Della.

Della who?

Dellacatessen is a tasty place to get some food.

Knock, knock.

Who's there?

Doughnut

Doughnut who?

Doughnut disturb me, I like my quiet time.

Knock, knock.

Who's there?

Sweden.

Sweden who?

Sweden the lemonade, it's too sour.

Knock, knock.

Who's there?

Jelly.

Jelly who?

Jellycopter, jellycopter.

Knock, knock.

Who's there?

Lettuce.

Lettuce who?

Lettuce in and you'll find out.

Knock, knock.

Who's there?

Loaf.

Loaf who?

I don't just like bread, I loaf it.

Knock, knock.

Who's there?

Eat.

Eat who?

Eat your veggies.

Knock, knock.

Who's there?

Muffin.

Muffin who?

Muffin the matter with me, how about you?

Knock, knock.

Who's there?

Ice cream.

Ice cream who?

Ice cream if you don't let me in.

Knock, knock.

Who's there?

Pudding.

Pudding who?

Pudding your shoes on before your pants is not a good idea.

Knock, knock.

Who's there?

Candy.

Candy who?

Candy cow jump over the moon?

Knock, knock.

Who's there?

Donut.

Donut who?

I donut know, you tell me.

Knock, knock.

Who's there?

Orange.

Orange who?

Orange you glad there is no school on Saturday?

Knock, knock.

Who's there?

Turnip.

Turnip who?

Turnip your doorbell volume, I've been ringing it forever.

Knock, knock.

Who's there?

Honeydew.

Honeydew who?

Honeydew your homework before you go outside.

Knock, knock.

Who's there?

Butter.

Butter who?

Butter bring an umbrella, it looks like rain.

Knock, knock.

Who's there?

Pudding.

Pudding who?

Pudding in your face.

Knock, knock.

Who's there?

Nacho.

Nacho who?

Nacho cheese, so give it back.

Knock, knock.

Who's there?

Leaf.

Leaf who?

Leaf me alone.

Knock, knock.

Who's there?

Cows go.

Cows go who?

Cows go moo, not who.

Knock, knock.

Who's there?

Hoo.

Hoo who?

You sure talk like an owl.

Knock, knock.

Who's there?

Goat.

Goat who?

Goat on a limb and open the door.

Knock, knock.

Who's there?

Lion.

Lion who?

Lion out in the sun on your doorstep, it's nice
outside.

Knock, knock.

Who's there?

Dragon.

Dragon who?

Dragon your feet again, hurry up and open the door.

Knock, knock.

Who's there?

Ducks.

Ducks who?

Ducks don't go who, they go quack.

Knock, knock.

Who's there?

Yorkies.

Yorkies who?

Yorkies don't fit in the lock.

Knock, knock.

Who's there?

Toucan.

Toucan who?

Toucan play that game.

Knock, knock.

Who's there?

Wood ant.

Wood ant who?

Wood ant you like to know.

Knock, knock.

Who's there?

Owls.

Owls who?

Exactly.

Knock, knock.

Who's there?

Hello.

Hello who?

Hello kitty.

Knock, knock.

Who's there?

Baby Owl.

Baby Owl who?

Baby, owl see you later.

Knock, knock.

Who's there?

Iguana.

Iguana who?

Iguana come in.

Knock, knock.

Who's there?

Safari.

Safari who?

Safari so good.

Knock, knock.

Who's there?

Flea.

Flea who?

Fleas a jolly good fellow.

Knock, knock.

Who's there?

Owl.

Owl who?

Owl aboard, the train is leaving.

Knock, knock.

Who's there?

Nana.

Nana who?

Nana your bee's wax.

Knock, knock.

Who's there?

Gopher.

Gopher who?

I could go for a cup of hot chocolate right about now.

Knock, knock.

Who's there?

Laughing tentacles.

Laughing tentacles who?

You would laugh too, if I gave you tentacles.

Knock, knock.

Who's there?

Quacker.

Quacker who?

Quacker another bad joke and I'm leaving.

Knock, knock.

Who's there?

Kanga.

Kanga who?

Close, it's kangaroo.

Knock, knock.

Who's there?

Herring.

Herring who?

Herring a lot of funny knock knock jokes today.

Knock, knock.

Who's there?

A cow with no lips.

A cow with no lips who?

A cow with no lips says ooo ooo.

Knock, knock.

Who's there?

Honey bee.

Honey bee who?

Honey, bee a good friend and let me in.

Knock, knock.

Who's there?

Thumpin'.

Thumpin' who?

Thumpin' green and slimy is crawling on your shoulder.

Knock, knock.

Who's there?

Henrietta.

Henrietta who?

Henrietta worm that was in his apple.

Knock, knock.

Who's there?

Wayne.

Wayne who?

Wayne, Wayne, go away, come again some other day.

Knock, knock.

Who's there?

Hello.

Hello who?

My name is not Who.

Knock, knock.

Who's there?

Sarah.

Sarah who?

Sarah way you could let me in?

Knock, knock.

Who's there?

Noah.

Noah who?

Noah good place to get a key for this door?

Knock, knock.

Who's there?

Heidi.

Heidi who?

Heidi-clare thumb war on you.

Knock, knock.

Who's there?

Harvey.

Harvey who?

How long Harvey going to play this game?

Knock, knock.

Who's there?

Irene.

Irene who?

Irene and Irene but still no one answers the door.

Knock, knock.

Who's there?

Queen.

Queen who?

Queen as a whistle.

Knock, knock.

Who's there?

Alex.

Alex who?

Just let me in, Alex-splain later.

Knock, knock.

Who's there?

Annie.

Annie who?

Annie time you want to open this door would be good.

Knock, knock.

Who's there?

Saul.

Saul who?

Saul the King's horses and all the King's men.

Knock, knock.

Who's there?

Stan.

Stan who?

Stan back, I'm about to open the door.

Knock, knock.

Who's there?

Toby.

Toby who?

Toby or not Toby, that is the question.

Knock, knock.

Who's there?

Sam.

Sam who?

Sam person who answered the door last time.

Knock, knock.

Who's there?

Karim.

Karim who?

Karim of the crop.

Knock, knock.

Who's there?

Wanda.

Wanda who?

Wanda where I put my car keys.

Knock, knock.

Who's there?

Wendy.

Wendy who?

Wendy door opens you'll find out.

Knock, knock.

Who's there?

Xavier.

Xavier who?

Xavier breath, I don't want to talk right now.

Knock, knock.

Who's there?

Leena.

Leena who?

Leena little closer and I will tell you.

Knock, knock.

Who's there?

Tinkerbell.

Tinkerbell who?

Think your bell is out of order, that's why I'm knocking.

Knock, knock.

Who's there?

Scott.

Scott who?

Scott nothing to do with you.

170

Knock, knock.

Who's there?

Adam.

Adam who?

Adam up and send me the bill.

Knock, Knock.

Who's there?

Abbey.

Abbey who?

A bee stung me on my bum.

Knock, knock.

Who's there?

Howie.

Howie who?

I'm fine, how are you?

9

More Random Funny Jokes

What kind of music do balloons hate?

Pop music.

Did you hear about the claustrophobic astronaut?

They just needed a little space.

Why are mountains so funny?

They're just hill areas.

Why did Billy get cut when he fell on the grass?

Because it's full of blades.

Why did the picture go to prison?

Because it was framed.

Why do bicycles fall over?

Because they're two-tired.

Why was the broom late?

It over-swept.

Where do sailboats go when they're sick?

To the dock.

What kind of water can't freeze?

Hot water.

Why didn't the shopper buy the camo pants they wanted?

They couldn't find any.

What did the family say when they lost 25% of their roof?

Oof.

Why are elevator jokes so good?

They work on many levels.

What do you call a boomerang that doesn't come back?

A stick.

Why are balloons so expensive?

Inflation.

Why was the calendar afraid?

Its days were numbered.

What do kids do during recess on rainy days?

Play bored games.

What's blue and smells like red paint?

Blue paint.

What's red and bad for your teeth?

A brick.

What did the zero say to the eight?

Nice belt.

What has ears but cannot hear?

A cornfield.

Can February March?

No, but April May.

What building in New York has the most stories?

The New York Public Library.

Why did it get so hot in the stadium after the game?

All the fans left.

What do you call a can opener that doesn't work?

A can't opener.

Why do we tell actors to "break a leg?"

Because every play has a cast.

Why did the lawyer show up in court in his underwear?

He forgot his lawsuit.

How did the beauty school student do on her manicure test?

She nailed it.

Why did the genie get mad?

Because he was rubbed the wrong way.

What should you wear to a tea party?

A t-shirt.

What's rain's favorite accessory?

A rainbow.

Where does a sink go dancing?

The dish-co.

What's the most popular video game at the bakery?

Knead for Speed.

What do you get if Santa goes down the chimney while the fire is lit?

Crisp Kringle.

Why is a cemetery a great place to write a story?

Because there are so many plots there.

Why was the equal sign so humble?

Because it wasn't greater than or less than anyone else.

Are any Halloween monsters good at math?

No - unless you Count Dracula.

How can you make a tissue dance?

Put a little boogie in it.

What do you call a train with a cold?

A-choo choo train.

What did the hair stylist name their dog?

Shampooch.

How do you talk to a giant?

Use big words.

What did the meteorologist say when they tried to catch fog?

I mist.

Why did the cell phone get glasses?

Because it lost all its contacts.

What runs around a baseball field but never moves?

A fence.

What musical instrument can you find in the bathroom?

A tuba toothpaste.

Why do bees have sticky hair?

They use honeycombs.

What do you call a droid that likes taking the scenic route?

R2-Detour.

Why is Cinderella so bad at playing football?

She runs away from the ball.

How do billboards talk to one another?

With sign language.

Why did Humpty Dumpty have a great fall?

To make up for his terrible summer.

What did the little boat say to the yacht?

"Can I interest you in a little row-mance?"

Where do twins go on vacation?

Pair-is.

I'm not mad that someone stole my flashlight.

I'm delighted.

A ride on a hot air balloon might not be the most incredible thing

ever, but it is up there.

My dad told me to get a new job skill, so I learned lockpicking.

It's opened a lot of doors for me.

Teachers love white boards. They are remarkable.

My friend didn't understand cloning.

I said that makes two of us.

What did the farmer call the cow that had no milk?

An udder failure.

Why are spiders so smart?

They can find everything on the web.

What's worse than finding a worm in your apple?

Finding half a worm in your apple.

What do you call bears with no ears?

B.

Why couldn't the pony talk?

Because she was just a little hoarse.

How do you keep a bull from charging?

Cancel its credit card.

Why did the pig have ink all over his face?

Because he just came out of the pen.

What do you get from a pampered cow?

Spoiled milk.

What do you call a hen who counts her eggs?

A mathema-chicken.

What kind of lion doesn't roar?

A dandelion.

What is black and white and red all over?

A zebra with a sunburn.

What kind of music do whales like?

They listen to the orca-stra.

What kind of jobs do funny chickens have?

They are comedy-hens.

What's the strongest type of sea creature?

Mussels.

What's a kitty cat's favorite color?

Purr-ple.

What kind of photos will you find on a turtle's phone?

Shell-fies.

What's a bee's normal haircut?

A buzz cut.

What do you get when you cross a centipede with a parrot?

A walkie talkie.

What do you call an illegally parked amphibian?

Toad.

What do you get when you cross a porcupine with a snail?

A slowpoke.

What breed of dog can jump higher than a skyscraper?

Any breed of dog. Skyscrapers can't jump.

What do you call a cow that can't moo?

A milk dud.

What do snakes like to study in school?

Hissss-tory.

Why are frogs stress-free?

They eat whatever bugs them.

What do cows order from?

Cattle-logs.

What creature is smarter than a talking parrot?

A spelling bee.

What's black and white and red all over?

A sunburned zebra.

What did the snail say when it rode on the turtle's back?

Wheeeee.

Where do sheep go to get their hair cut?

The baa-baa shop.

Which bird is always out of breath?

A puffin.

How does a cucumber become a pickle?

It goes through a jarring experience.

Why oranges wear sunscreen?

So they don't peel.

Why did the student eat his homework?

Because his teacher said it was a piece of cake.

Why do we put candles on top of birthday cakes?

Because it's hard to light them from the bottom.

What do you call a retired vegetable?

A has-bean.

Why did the baker put the cake in the freezer?

She wanted to ice it.

Where do you learn to make banana splits?

At sundae school.

What kind of fruit do twins love the most?

Pears.

What do they serve for breakfast on flights?

Plane bagels.

What do cowboys put on their salads?

Ranch dressing.

Where do hamburgers go dancing?

A meat ball.

What kind of vegetable is angry?

A steamed carrot.

What vegetable do sailors never want on their boats?

Leeks.

Why did the teacher draw on the window?

Because he wanted his lesson to be very clear.

186

What's a pirate's favorite class to take in school?

Arrrt.

What did the school librarian say when a book fell on their head?

I have only my shelf to blame.

How did the student feel when he learned about electricity?

Totally shocked.

Why did the bikes get detention at school?

They spoke too much.

Why didn't anyone want to eat next to the basketball team?

Because they dribble too much.

10

Even More Knock Knock Jokes

Knock, knock.

Who's there?

John Cena.

John Cena who?

John Cena spider, now he's running scared.

Knock, knock.

Who's there?

Will.

Will who?

Will you let me in, its cold out here.

Knock, knock.

Who's there?

Barbie.

Barbie who?

Barbie Q Chicken is delicious.

Knock, knock.

Who's there?

Ken.

Ken who?

Ken you please open the door, Barbie?

Knock, knock.

Who's there?

Alda.

Alda who?

Alda good knock knock jokes are here, right?

Knock, knock.

Who's there?

Teresa.

Teresa who?

Teresa way to find out who I am, open the door.

Knock, knock.

Who's there?

Alli.

Alli who?

Alligator, that's who.

Knock, knock.

Who's there?

Hollis.

Hollis who?

Hollis not lost, we can still win.

Knock, knock.

Who's there?

Hugo.

Hugo who?

Hugo that way, and I'll go this way.

Knock, knock.

Who's there?

Isabelle.

Isabelle who?

Isabelle out of order? I had to knock.

Knock, knock.

Who's there?

Avery.

Avery who?

Avery time I come to your house we go through this.

Knock, knock.

Who's there?

Barry.

Barry who?

Barry the treasure in the backyard.

Knock, knock.

Who's there?

Ben.

Ben who?

Ben knocking so long my hand hurts.

Knock, knock.

Who's there?

Dewey.

Dewey who.

Dewey have to listen to all this knocking?

Knock, knock.

Who's there?

Doris.

Doris who?

Doris locked, that's why I'm knocking.

Knock, knock.

Who's there?

Douglas.

Douglas who?

Is da glass half empty or half full?

Knock, knock.

Who's there?

Felix.

Felix who?

Feel exhausted, let me in so I can rest.

Knock, knock.

Who's there?

Harmony.

Harmony who?

Harmony times do I have to tell you?

Knock, knock.

Who's there?

Harriet.

Harriet who?

Harriet up, and open the door.

Knock, knock.

Who's there?

Hayden.

Hayden who?

Do you wanna play Hayden seek?

Knock, knock.

Who's there?

Ivan.

Ivan who?

Ivan extremely sore hand from knocking.

Knock, knock.

Who's there?

Joe.

Joe who?

Joe King with you.

Knock, knock.

Who's there?

Ken.

Ken who?

Ken you tell me some good knock knock jokes?

Knock, knock.

Who's there?

Rhoda.

Rhoda who?

Row, row, Rhoda boat.

Knock, knock.

Who's there?

Shelby.

Shelby who?

Shelby comin' round the mountain when she comes.

Knock, knock.

Who's there?

Shirley.

Shirley who?

Shirley you must know me by now.

Knock, knock.

Who's there?

Stu.

Stu who?

Stu late to ask questions.

Knock, knock.

Who's there?

Theodore.

Thedore who?

Theodore is shut, please open it.

Knock, knock.

Who's there?

Candace.

Candace who?

Candace day get any better? No.

Knock, knock.

Who's there?

Pecan.

Pecan who?

Pecan somebody your own size.

Knock, knock.

Who's there?

Hungry clock.

Hungry clock who?

Hungry clock who went back four seconds.

Knock, knock.

Who's there?

Closure.

Closure who?

Closure mouth while you're chewing.

Knock, knock.

Who's there?

Bean.

Bean who?

Bean a while since I last saw ya.

Knock, knock.

Who's there?

Egg.

Egg who?

Egg-cited to see me?

Knock, knock.

Who's there?

Four Eggs.

Four Eggs who?

Four Eggs sample.

Knock, knock.

Who's there?

Handsome.

Handsome who?

Handsome pizza to me please.

Knock, knock.

Who's there?

Ketchup.

Ketchup who?

Ketchup with me and I'll tell you.

Knock, knock.

Who's there?

Pasta.

Pasta who?

Pasta parmesan please.

Knock, knock.

Who's there?

Banana.

Banana who?

Banana split so it's just me.

Knock, knock.

Who's there?

Jalapeno.

Jalapeno who?

Am I getting jalapeno business?

Knock, knock.

Who's there?

Two 4's

Two 4's who?

No need to make lunch, we already 8.

Knock, knock.

Who's there?

Pizza.

Pizza who?

Pete's a really great guy.

Knock, knock.

Who's there?

Omelette.

Omelette who?

Omelette smarter than I look.

Knock, knock.

Who's there?

Avocado.

Avocado who?

Avocado cold.

Knock, knock.

Who's there?

Cash.

Cash who?

Oh, no, you're sick, too.

Knock, knock.

Who's there?

Falafel.

Falafel who?

Falafel off my bike and hurt my knee.

Knock, knock.

Who's there?

Turnip.

Turnip who?

Turnip your doorbell volume, I've been ringing it forever.

Knock, knock.

Who's there?

Carrot.

Carrot who?

Do you even carrot all?

Knock, knock.

Who's there?

Donut.

Donut who?

I donut know. You tell me.

Knock, knock.

Who's there?

Déjav.

Déjav who?

Knock, knock.

Knock, knock.

Who's there?

Island.

Island who?

Island on your roof by accident when I parachuted.

Knock, knock.

Who's there?

Aloha.

Aloha who?

Aloha myself down from your roof.

Knock, knock.

Who's there?

Hawaii.

Hawaii who?

I'm fine, how are you?

Knock, knock.

Who's there?

Amusing.

Amusing who?

Amusing your doorbell, but it doesn't work.

Knock, knock.

Who's there?

Avenue.

Avenue who?

Avenue heard the news? Open up.

Knock, knock.

Who's there?

Francis.

Francis who?

Francis is in Europe.

Knock, knock.

Who's there?

Europe.

Europe who?

Europe late.

Knock, knock.

Who's there?

Pasture.

Pasture who?

It's pasture bedtime, go to sleep.

Knock, knock.

Who's there?

Deluxe.

Deluxe, who?

Deluxe broken, I can't use my key.

Knock, knock.

Who's there?

Icy.

Icy who?

I see you haven't fixed your doorbell yet.

Knock, knock.

Who's there?

Juicy.

Juicy who?

Juicy this funny video on YouTube? It's hilarious.

Knock, knock.

Who's there?

Kenya.

Kenya who?

Kenya open the door, it's raining out here.

Knock, knock.

Who's there?

Alpaca.

Alpaca who?

Alpaca the suitcase, you load up the car.

Knock, knock.

Who's there?

Ash.

Ash Who?

I did not mean to make you sneeze.

Knock, knock.

Who's there?

Wiper.

Wiper who?

Wiper nose, it's running.

Knock, knock.

Who's there?

Tish.

Tish who?

Here you go, wipe your nose.

Knock, knock.

Who's there?

Moose.

Moose who?

Moose you be so nosy?

Knock, knock.

Who's there?

Cook.

Cook who?

I'm not crazy, you are.

Knock, knock.

Who's there?

Thermos.

Thermos who?

Thermos be a better knock knock joke than this.

Knock, knock.

Who's there?

Bach.

Bach who?

Bach, Bach, Bach, I'm a chicken.

Knock, knock.

Who's there?

Hammond.

Hammond who?

Hammond eggs for breakfast please.

Knock, knock.

Who's there?

Olive.

Olive who?

I love you, too.

Knock, knock.

Who's there?

Isma

Isma who?

Isma lunch ready yet.

Knock, knock.

Who's there?

Althea.

Althea who?

Althea later alligator.

Knock, knock.

Who's there?

Dimitri.

Dimitri who?

Dimitri is where hamburgers grow.

Knock, knock.

Who's there?

Adelia.

Adelia who?

Adelia the cards and we'll play Crazy Eights.

Knock, knock.

Who's there?

Dawn.

Dawn who?

Dawn leave me out here in the cold.

Knock, knock.

Who's there?

Anita.

Anita who?

Anita 'nother tissue.

Knock, knock.

Who's there?

Sore ewe.

Sore ewe who?

Sore ewe gonna open the door or not?

Knock, knock.

Who's there?

Aldo.

Aldo who?

Aldo it's raining, you can still come outside.

Knock, knock.

Who's there?

Amanda

Amanda who?

Amanda repair your doorbell.

Knock, knock.

Who's there?

Hello.

Hello who?

My name's not who.

Knock, knock.

Who's there?

Porpoise.

Porpoise who?

For all intents and porpoises the case is closed.

Knock, knock.

Who's there?

Chicken.

Chicken who?

Chicken to see how you are doing.

Knock, knock.

Who's there?

Guitar playing tuna.

Guitar playing tuna who?

Don't be silly, you can't tuna fish.

Knock, knock.

Who's there?

Door-bell repair man.

Doorbell repair man who?

No, seriously, I'm here to repair your doorbell.

Knock, knock.

Who's there?

Alfredo sauce.

Alfredo sauce who?

Alfredo sauce so many people waiting, he went home.

Knock, knock.

Who's there?

Diesel.

Diesel who?

Diesel be a good day to go for a walk in the park.

Knock, knock.

Who's there?

Dozen.

Dozen who?

Dozen anyone recognize my voice anymore?

Knock, knock.

Who's there?

Knock knock.

Who's there?

No, you're supposed to say, "Knock knock, who?"

Knock, knock.

Who's there?

Easily distracted pirate.

Easily distracted pirate who?

Arrr, look, a squirrel!

Knock, knock.

Who's there?

Riot.

Riot, who?

Riot on time, you're here.

Knock, knock.

Who's there?

A boat.

A boat, who?

A boat time you answered the door.

Knock, knock.

Who's there?

Disguise.

Disguise, who?

Disguise de limit.

Knock, knock.

Who's there?

Sword.

Sword, who?

Sword of easy to find out, just open the door.

Knock, knock.

Who's there?

Wire.

Wire, who?

Wire you making me wait outside, let me in.

Knock, knock.

Who's there?

Waddle.

Waddle who?

Waddle we do for fun today?

Knock, knock.

Who's there?

Windy.

Windy who?

Windy you think you can come out to play?

Knock, knock.

Who's there?

Wooden shoe.

Wooden shoe who?

Wooden shoe like to know.

Knock, knock.

Who's there?

Yacht.

Yacht who?

Yacht to be happy, I'm here to visit

Knock, knock.

Who's there?

Your best friend.

Your best friend who?

Come on, you know your own best friend.

Knock, knock.

Who's there?

Impatient pirate.

Impatient pirat-

(Interrupting) Arrrrrrrh!

Knock, knock.

Who's there?

Deluxe.

Deluxe, who?

Deluxe Ness Monster.

Knock, knock.

Who's there?

Honey bee.

Honey bee who?

Honey bee a nice person and let me in.

Knock, knock.

Who's there?

A broken pencil.

A broken pencil who?

Forget it, there's no point.

Knock, knock.

Who's there?

Alaska.

Alaska who?

Alaska if you can come over to play.

Knock, knock.

Who's there?

Goat.

Goat who?

Goat side, it's sunny and warm.

Knock, knock.

Who's there?

Déjav.

Déjav who?

Knock, knock.

11

Bonus Jokes

LIL MAC'S JOKE:

Where do cats go to recycle?

The litter box.

What's the strongest vegetable?

Muscle sprouts.

I saw a baguette at the zoo.

It was bread in captivity.

What happens if you eat yeast and shoe polish?

Every morning you'll rise and shine.

What is the most hardworking part of the eye?

The pupil.

What do you call the security working outside Samsung shops?

Guardians of the Galaxy.

What do you get when you cross a cow and a duck?

Milk and quackers.

What did the leopard say after eating his owner?

Wow, that hit the spot.

Why is your foot more special than your other body parts?

Because they have their own soul.

Why do fish live in salt water?

Because pepper makes them sneeze.

Why did the man put his money in the freezer?

He wanted cold hard cash.

What is the best day to go to the beach?

Sunday, of course.

What bow can't be tied?

A rainbow.

People ask me why I tuck my knees into my chest and lean forward.

That's just how I roll.

Why did the birdie go to the hospital?

To get a tweetment.

What did one elevator say to the other elevator?

I think I'm coming down with something.

What never asks questions but is answered a lot?

The telephone.

What kind of button won't unbutton?

A bellybutton.

What did the judge say when the skunk walked in the court room?

Odor in the court.

How do you find a Cinderella if you have her shoe?

You follow the foot Prince.

Why did the boy sprinkle sugar on his pillow before he went to sleep?

So he could have sweet dreams.

What did the judge say to the dentist?

Do you swear to pull the tooth, the whole tooth, and nothing but the tooth.

Why did the computer break up with the internet?

There was no connection.

What do you call a book that's about the brain?

A mind reader.

When do you stop at green and go at red?

When you're eating a watermelon.

What do you call a teacher who never farts in public?

A private tutor.

Why was the math book sad?

Because it had too many problems.

Why can't a leopard hide?

Because he's always spotted.

What happened to the wooden car with wooden wheels and a wooden engine?

It wooden go.

Why did the tree go to the dentist?

To get a root canal.

What four letters will stop a burglar?

O-I-C-U.

What's the difference between a cat and a frog?

A cat has nine lives but a frog croaks every night.

There's a new restaurant called Karma.

There's no menu, they just give you what you deserve.

What do you get when you cross a bear and skunk?

Winnie the Pee-yew.

What's the biggest moth in the world?

A mam-moth.

What's the last thing you take off, before you go to bed?

Your take your feet off the floor.

Who can shave six times a day, and still have a full beard?

A barber.

Why is camping an extreme sport?

Cause it's in tents.

What do you call a rich elf?

Welfy.

What do birds give out on Halloween?

Tweets.

How do mountains stay warm in winter?

Snowcaps.

Why did the man run around his bed?

He was trying to catch up on sleep.

Why do dragons sleep during the day?

So they can fight knights.

Where do cows go for entertainment?

To the moo-vies.

What kind of fish will only swim at night?

A starfish.

If frozen water is iced water and if frozen lemonade is iced lemonade, then what's frozen ink called?

Iced ink.

No, you don't smell that bad.

I'm going to stand outside. So if anyone asks, I am outstanding.

I'm so bright my mother calls me son.

I am going bananas. That's what I say to my bananas before I leave the house.

Change is hard. Have you ever tried to bend a quarter?

If money doesn't grow on trees why do banks have branches?

I can't believe I got fired from the calendar factory. All I did was take a day off.

I wonder if earth makes fun of other planets for having no life.

It's been scientifically proven that too many birthdays can kill you.

I love pressing F5 while on the internet browser. It's so refreshing.

Knock, knock.

Who's there?

Déjà.

Déjà who?

Knock, knock.

Acknowledgments

Special thank you to all of our friends who share jokes with us!

Thank you for reading our book! We hope you enjoyed it and laughed out loud.

Please tell these jokes to your friends and family and make more people happy.

If you liked this book, we'd love it if you gave us a good rating at whatever store you bought it from.

About The Authors

The Hennessy Kids think the world would be better with more smiles.

Katherine, Daniel, and Samuel, known as The Hennessy Kids, are #1 Kobo Canada bestsellers for kids joke books.

Want to know when more fun stuff like this is available? Sign up for the **Fun Stuff With Heart** newsletter at HennessyEnt.com.

Books By The Hennessy Kids

101 Halloween Jokes

101 Christmas Jokes

101 Pet Jokes

101 Knock Knock Jokes, Vol. 1

101 Nature Jokes

101 Food Jokes

101 Funny Jokes, Vol. 1

101 Knock Knock Jokes, Vol. 2

101 Knock Knock Jokes, Vol. 3

101 Funny Jokes, Vol. 2

The Big Book Of Jokes

Visit hennessyent.com for the complete & up-to-date list of fun books!

If you borrowed this book from your local public library or your school library, you could ask to read more of our books, too. And thank you for visiting your library!